I0073618

THE BOOK Business Boss®

WHAT IS A BOOK BUSINESS BOSS?

A BOOK BUSINESS BOSS IS DEFINED AS SOMEONE WHO IS AN AUTHOR, PUBLISHER, ILLUSTRATOR, GRAPHIC DESIGNER, EDITOR, LAYOUT ARTIST, BOOK PROMOTER OR MARKETER THAT SEEKS TO INFLUENCE, CONTRIBUTE AND DOMINATE IN THE LITERARY WORLD.

All Books listed in the magazine can be purchased in print or ebook formats via major distribution outlets.

For more information or to advertise

Mail: P. O. Box 4321 | Jeffersonville, IN 47131

Phone: 502.694.2143

Email: bookbusinessboss@gmail.com

ISBN: 978-1-971868-02-8

ROYSTON ROYAL
BOOKSTORE

Books. Gifts and More.

http://www.roystonroyalbookstore.com

We are pleased to announce the opening of the BK Royston Publishing and Royal Media and Publishing combined online store with books, gifts, monthly subscription book boxes, resources for homeschoolers, teaching aids and other merchandise.

Bringing it all in one place. We still have the multi-week courses at http://www.bkroystonstore.com but now the books can be purchased under one banner at http://www.roystonroyalbookstore.com.

Supplying you with books, gifts and merchandise fit for royalty.

Table of Contents

Graphics for Covers

Bill Lacy
Jonathan Snorten
DesignArtist
Gad of Elite Covers
FX and Color Studio

Photographers

Joe Goodwin
Jonathan Snorten
Shannon Drummond

Production
Brian K. Royston

FROM THE EDITOR

The Next PIVOT

It's time to pivot again. I hate change just like the next person but when you can see the handwriting on the wall, the movement of the economy, the societal redefinition of work, the impact it could have on money and business plus the state of world, you pivot. Can't wait on everything to HAPPEN. We've got to PREPARE ourselves for what COULD happen. I know that we learned this word during 2020 or the COVID crisis but I don't think that COVID or the word pivot is going away any time soon. So, what does pivot really mean to me? I'm so glad that you asked. As a former marching band piccolo player, when it was time to change direction, you got on the right/correct foot and made that turn as smooth and sharp as ever. We didn't announce it but we had specific instructions, all summer to learn the steps and every day during and after school to perfect it all while to the beat of the music. Bring that same idea to today.

Figure out what music/beat/passion/gift/talent is moving you and your life. Ask God for specific instructions. Make that turn if your life as equipped, informed, smooth and sharp as possible. Your pivot will look different than others. Your pivot may look crazy to others.

Some people will exit and others will enter with the next pivot. With God's help, His map, your movement and keeping your momentum, you'll arrive exactly where you're supposed to be and on time too.

Now, ask yourself:
Do I want to be in this same place this time next year?
What does my heart say about where I am?
What does God say about where I am now or where I should be?
What do I need to do now to get to where God wants me to be?
The answers to these questions are left up to you but in the end, seek God. Get His direction and then move, adjust, purge, learn, grow and somehow PIVOT. In the end, let's go!

JULIA A. ROYSTON

Author, Publisher and Coach
www.talkwithroyston.com
www.juliaakroyston.com
bkroystonpublishing@gmail.com

Book Business Boss

Podcast

Julia A. Royston, Host
www.juliaakroyston.com

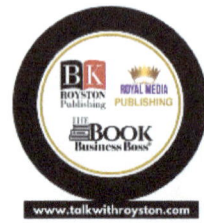

Subscribe at:
www.bookbusinessbosspodcast.com

Memoirs: Your Life Story

For years and even now, I tell people that they should write and tell their story. Some of their life stories are traumatic, painful and triggering. I now realize that I need to tell people that their story can be impactful, transformation and inspirational to others BUT they have to prepare themselves before beginning that journey. Why?

1.   You have to prepare yourself mentally, physically and emotionally for reliving some of those moments and situations in time. They can be triggering and traumatizing to you and open old wounds that you thought were healed.

2.   You may need a therapist to help you on that journey. I am understanding, helpful with the writing process but not certified or qualified to walk you through that process. I have seen it happen to too many clients. Business wise, I would prefer that you be finished with the book's first draft than to start you off from scratch. Why? Because sometimes the writing causes you to stop and never return to the manuscript.

3.   Writing is within itself emotional. Even if you're writing fiction and it is not related to your personal story, it is still emotional. You have to put yourself in the place of your character and determine how they feel, what they say and ultimately, what they do.

4. I became addicted to writing because my first book was journalled out of pain, disappointment, divorce and loss. I was healing through the words on that 80 count notebook from the dollar store even known of the poems were about what I had been through only the future. I filled 5 to 10 of those notebooks before my actual book was published. I didn't publish my first book until I remarried, God told me it was time, I had music to go along with the poetry, I had people who supported me and my husband supported me 1000% on the journey to publishing. It was time.

5. Finally, get ready, be ready and spiritually and emotionally, prepare yourself for the journey.

These steps apply to those suffering grief or writing about someone who they loved who passed away. It is an emotional journey and I'll go through it as much as possible but I can't do it all for you. My job is to be sympathetic, understanding and supportive but also my job is a business, taken seriously and if you're not ready, just say so.

Finally, there is someone who is in a worst place, has questions and you have experienced the steps they need to get out, never go into that situation or warn others about the potentials of the horrible situation. Prepare yourself but don't let fear, past trauma or current trauma stop you from the healing that you need while helping someone get healed in the process. This is a two-way process. Others are blessed but you are blessed and continue further on the journey to wholeness in the process.

When you're ready, LET'S TALK. www.talkwithroyston.com

Children's Book Self-Study Course

CHILDREN'S

TWEENS/TEENS

Create Great Children's Books
Purchase at: juliaroystonstore.com

THE BOOK Business Boss®

The Book Business Boss is a Registered Trademark!

Ready to Be a Book Business Boss

visit:
www.bookbusinessboss.com

Subscribe:
Youtube Channel @bookbusinessboss
www.bookbusinessbosspodcast.com

What can that mean for your book, business and industry? Let's find out by scheduling a conversation at:
www.talkwithroyston.com

Let's go!

Promote that Book Now! Book Promotion Tip

Your book or intellectual property as it is called in the legal community is valuable and doesn't lose its value or mold like bread. The oldest book that has sold the most is STILL the Bible and being printed every single year. Your book is a couple of years old, so what! My first book is about to be 19 years old. I print some every year especially places that I have NEVER been before.

NOTHING is guaranteed but if no one knows about your book, then how can they know to buy it.

My motto is:
New People = New Profits
More Products +New Places = More Profits

When was the last time that you promoted your book? When was the last you attend an event in a new city, new place and to people who do NOT know you.

Don't put away your book but look for new places for your book to positioned and seen. Don't down play the book that you've written because one man's book is another man's foundation to an empire.

If you need me, let's talk! Schedule a conversation at www.talkwithroyston.com. Let's go!

Promote that Book Now! Instant Access Course

PROMOTE THAT BOOK NOW INSTANT ACCESS COURSE!

Julia A. Royston

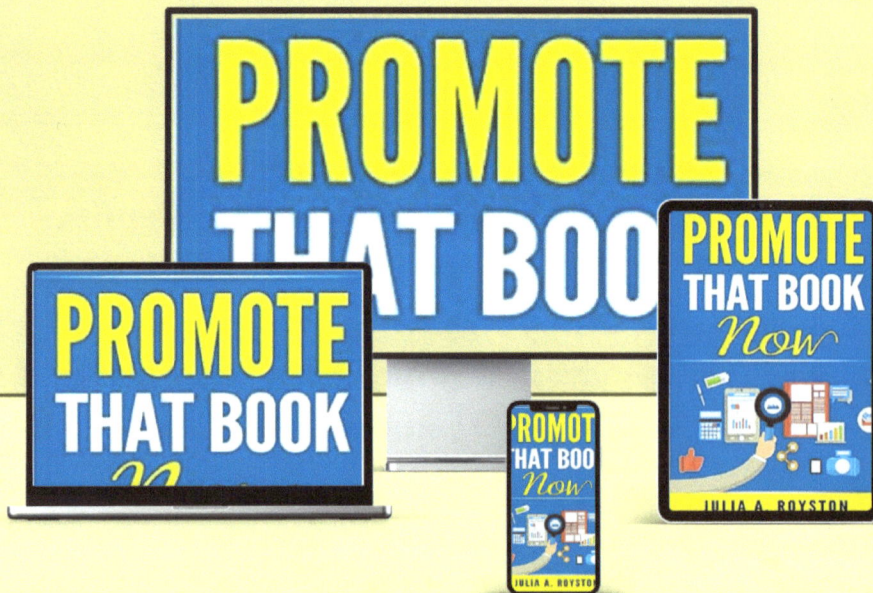

PROMOTE THAT BOOK

PROMOTE THAT BOOK

PROMOT THAT BOO Now

PROMOTE THAT BOOK Now

JULIA A. ROYSTON

REGISTER AT WWW.JULIAROYSTONSTORE.COM

Learn Online.
Anywhere. Anytime.

Royston Instant Access Courses

www.juliaroystonstore.com

Learn Anywhere.
Learn Anytime.

www.juliaroystonstore.com

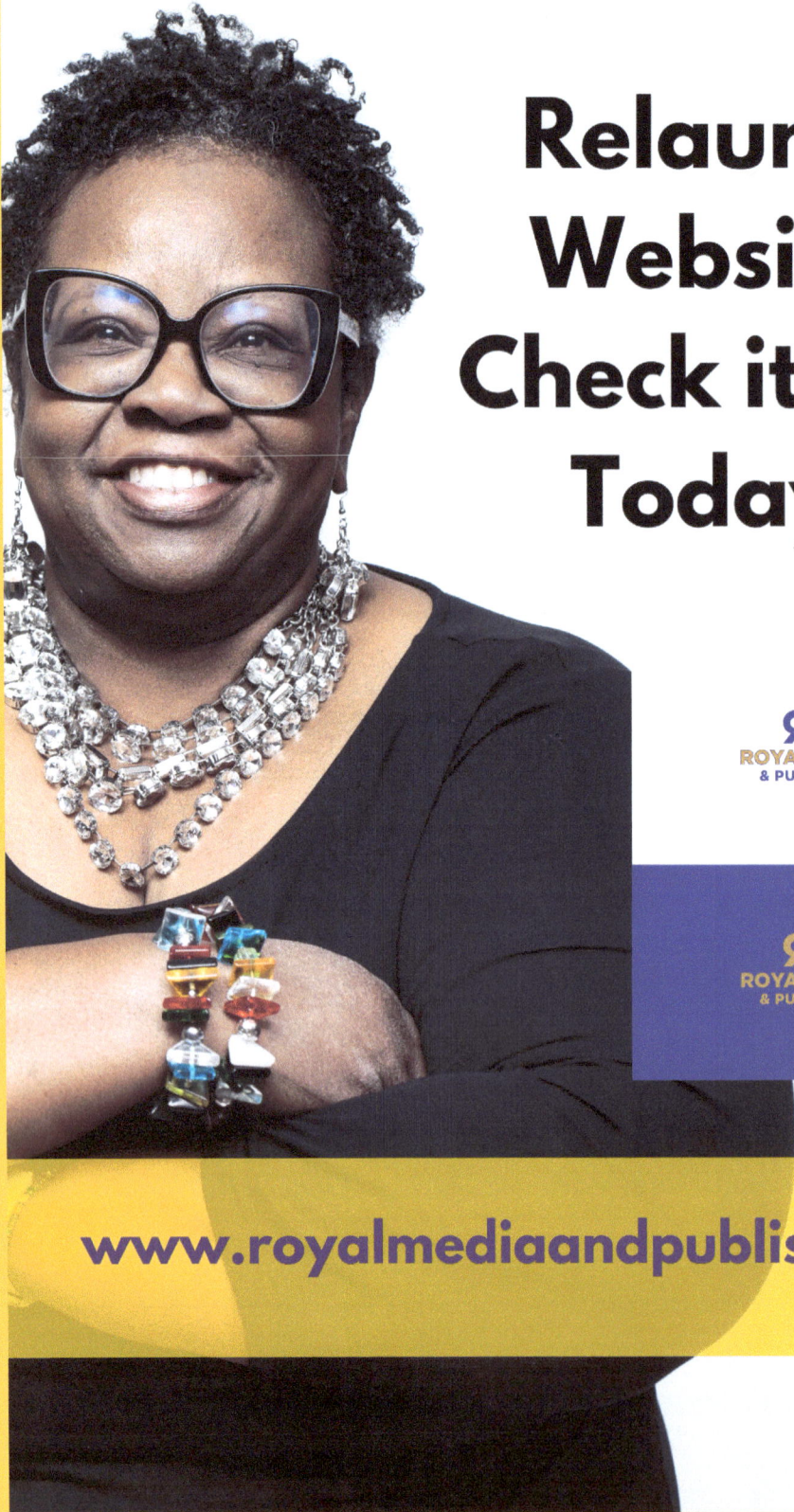

Relaunch Website! Check it Out Today!

ROYAL MEDIA
& PUBLISHING

ROYAL MEDIA
& PUBLISHING

www.royalmediaandpublishing.com

New Releases..

Support these authors, follow them on social media and purchase their books via www.amazon.com

Giovanni Bass

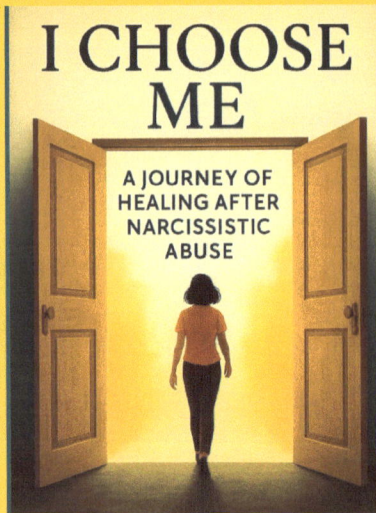

Wendell Bowen

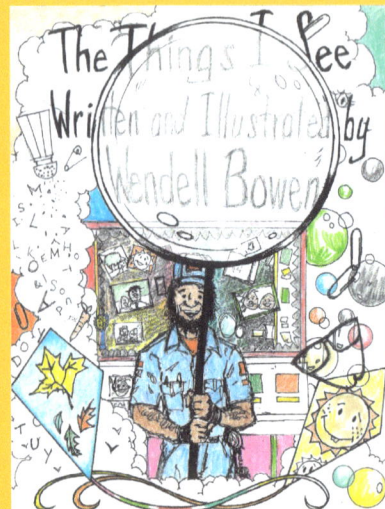

Bishop L. Lawrence Brandon

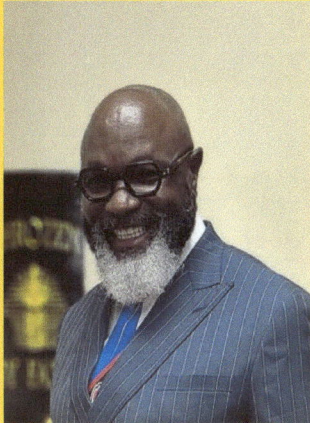

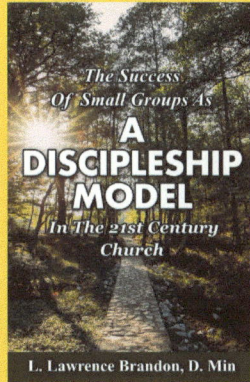

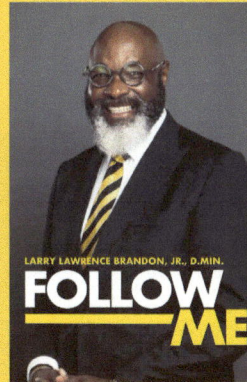

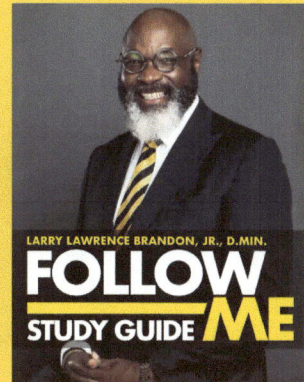

Ambassador
Pamela Bridgewater

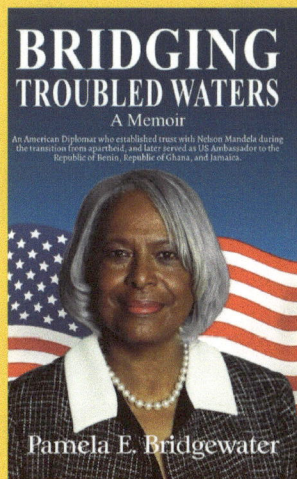

Rochea Brown & Kyle Shook

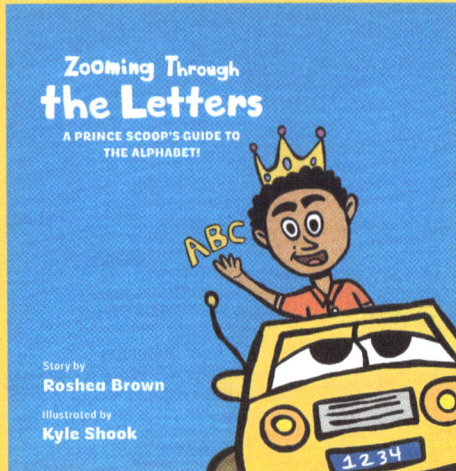

Tasha Bryant

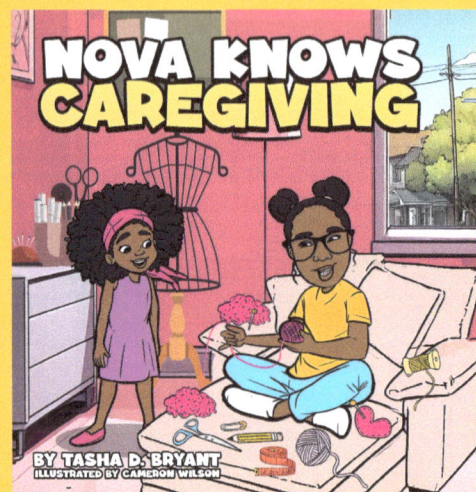

Tricia Delice

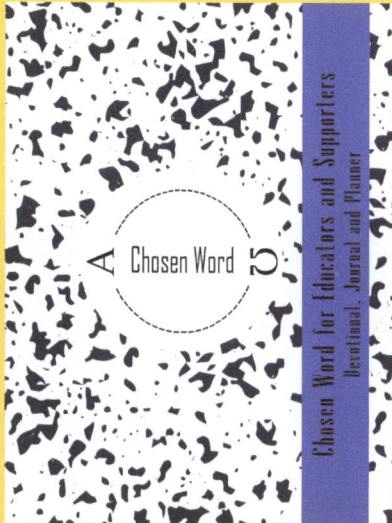

Juanita Edmondson

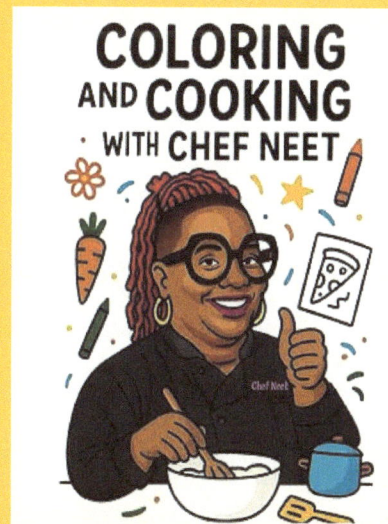

Boyd English

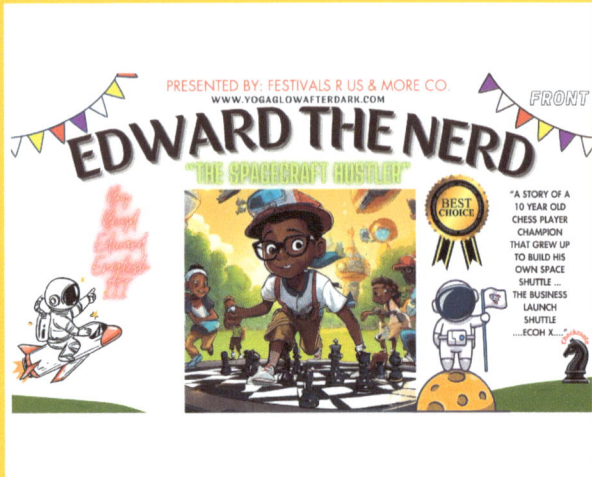

Delena Ferguson

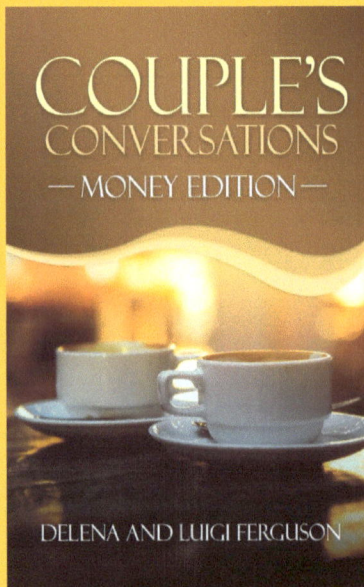

Elizabeth Gore

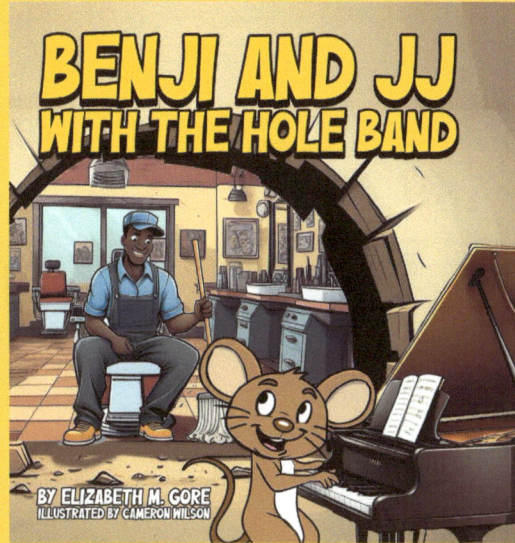

Dr. Tasha Griffith

Dr. Robert O'Keefe Hassell

Brandy Hatcher

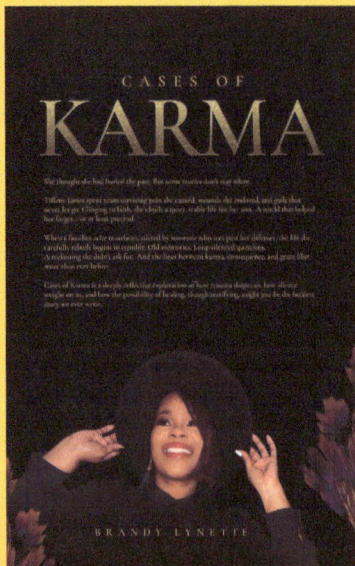

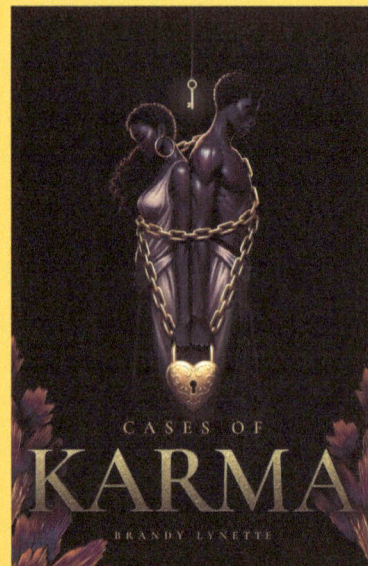

Charla V. Johnson

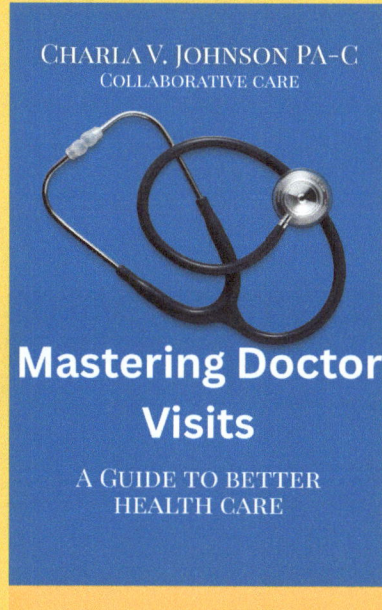

CHARLA V. JOHNSON PA-C
COLLABORATIVE CARE

Mastering Doctor Visits

A GUIDE TO BETTER HEALTH CARE

D.E. Maddox

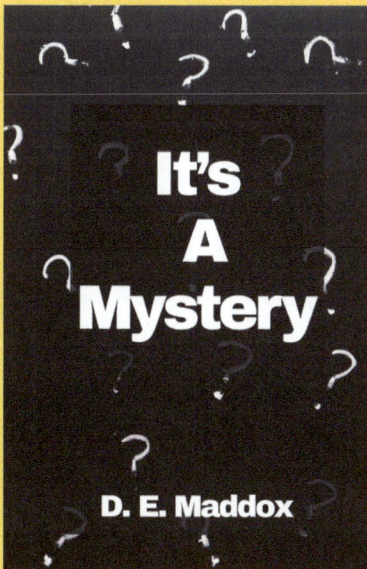

It's
A
Mystery

D. E. Maddox

Dr. John Marshall

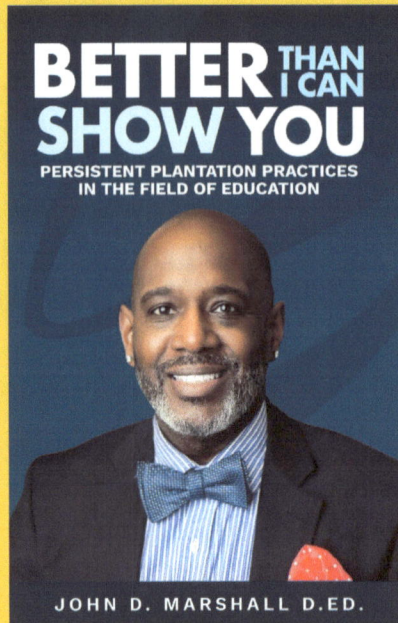

S. S. Miller

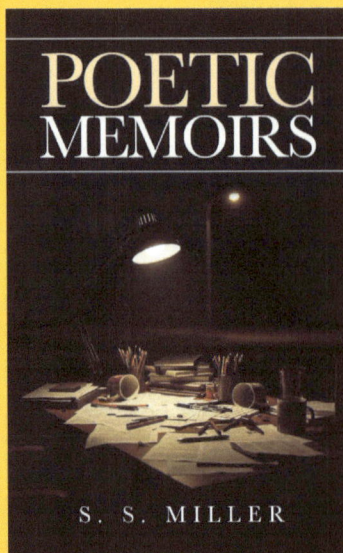 

Deborah Moss

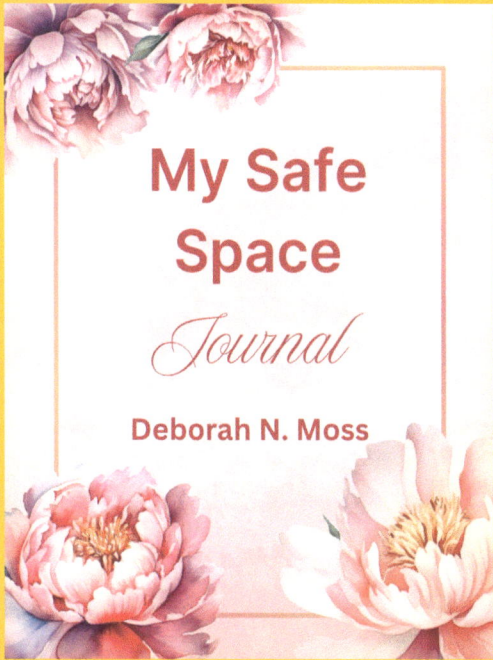

Les F. Murphy

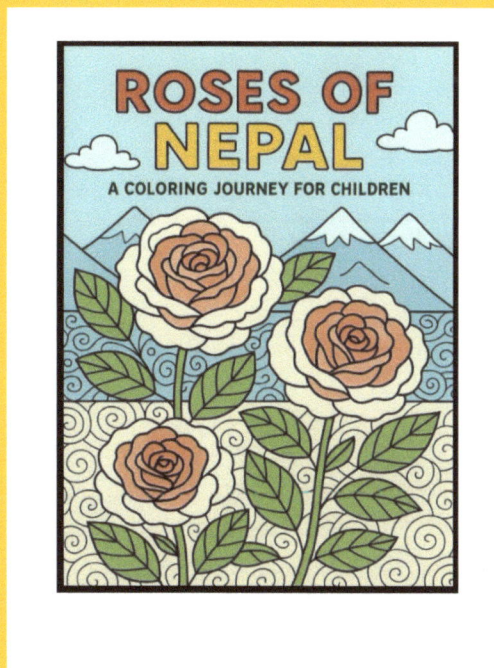

Gina Patterson

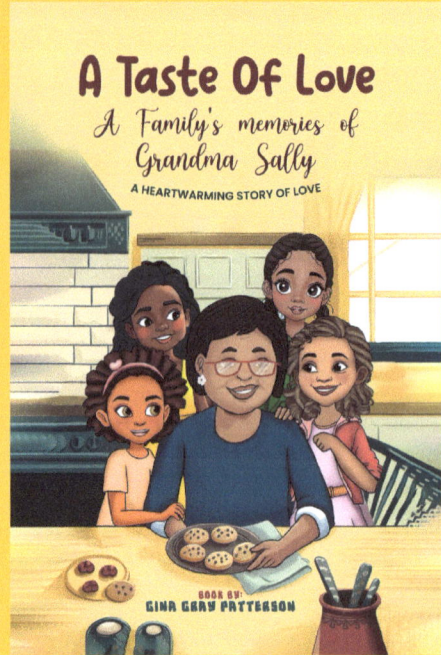

Kierra Patterson

Jeanette C. Pope

Oliver Rankine

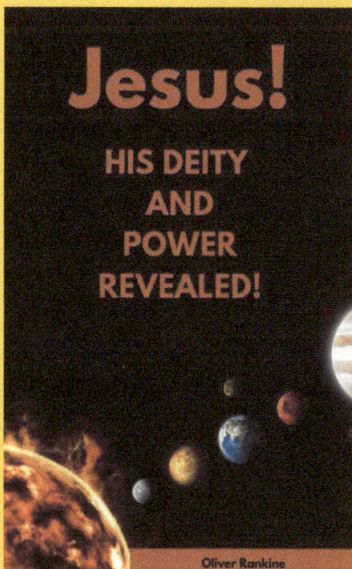

Sonya Moran Royston

Dr. Janet Seay-Stanley

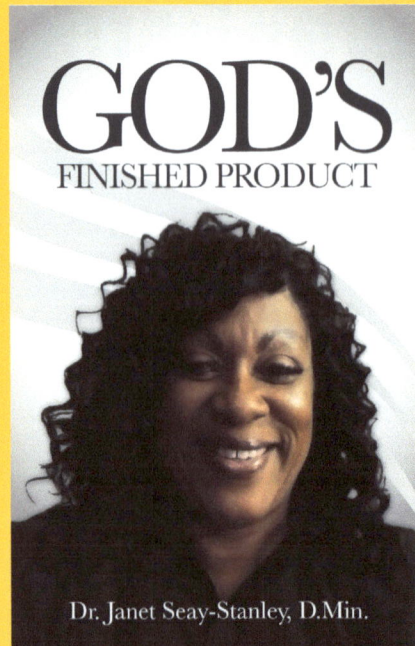

Joanne Lett-Sellers

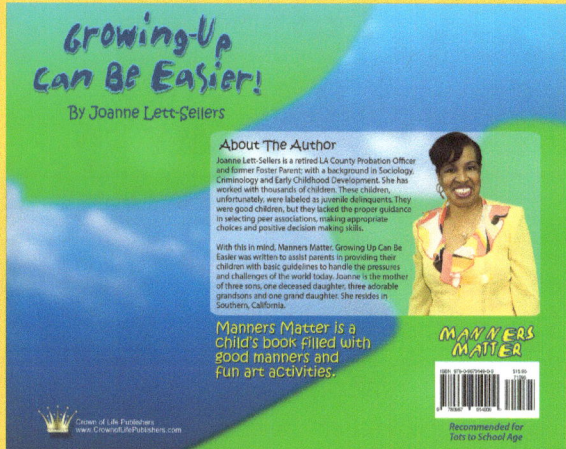

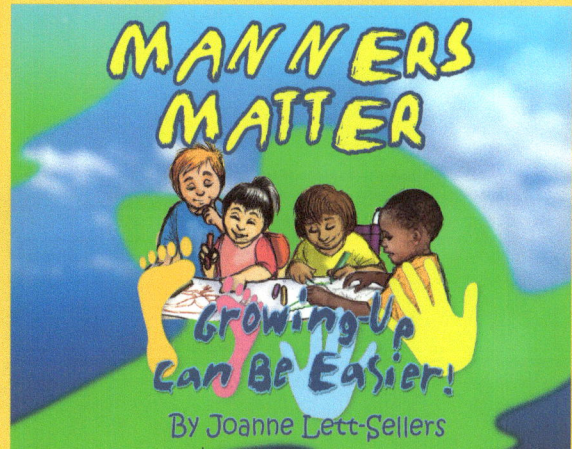

Dr. Daemon Stevenson

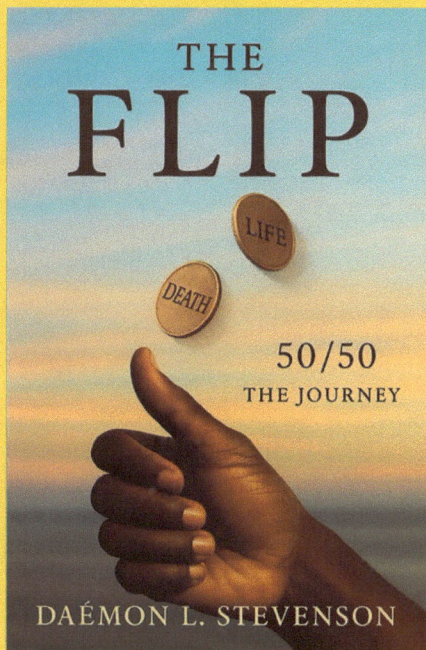

Karen Thompson

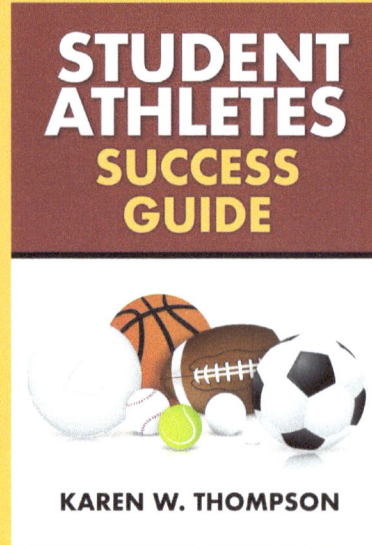

Cynthia Turner

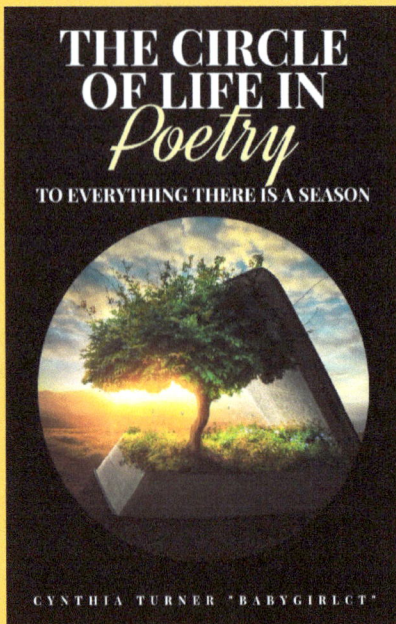

Angela Verges

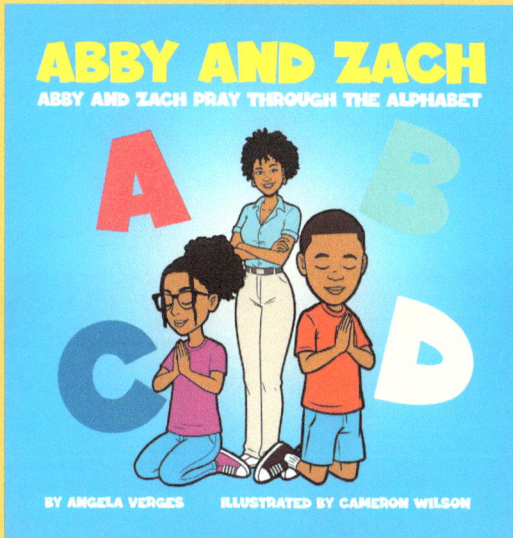

Dr. Ruth Wilson

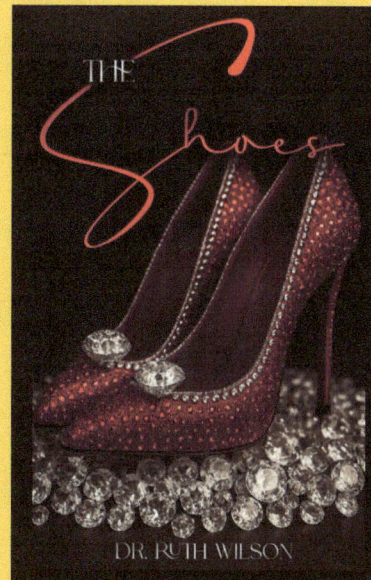

Don Wood

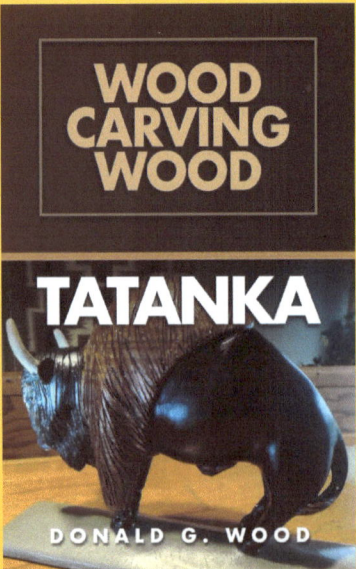

WOOD CARVING WOOD

TATANKA

DONALD G. WOOD

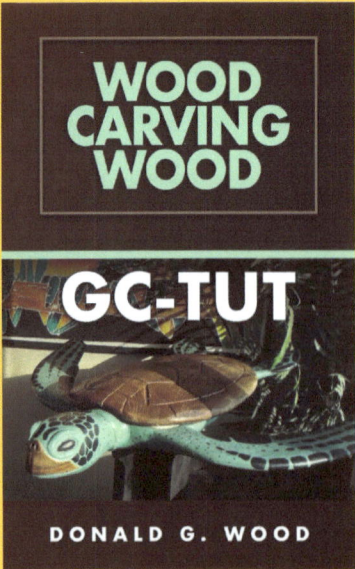

WOOD CARVING WOOD

GC-TUT

DONALD G. WOOD

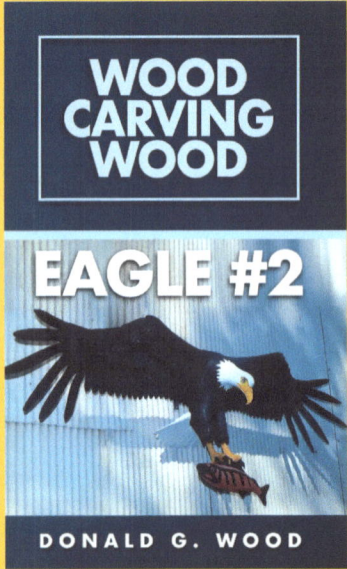

WOOD CARVING WOOD

EAGLE #2

DONALD G. WOOD

Julia A. Royston

Author. Publisher. Coach. Consultant

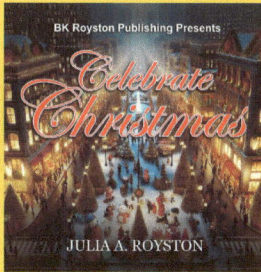

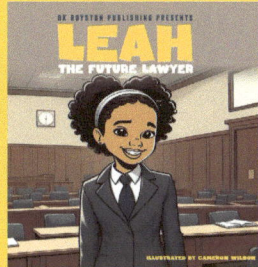

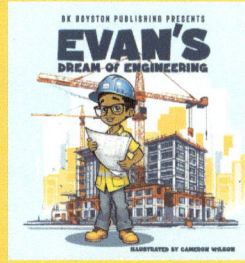

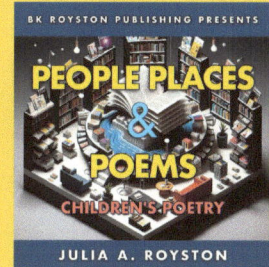

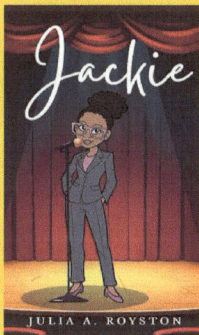

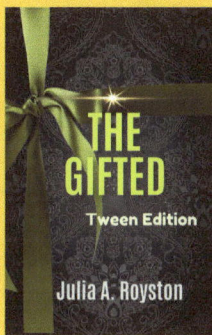

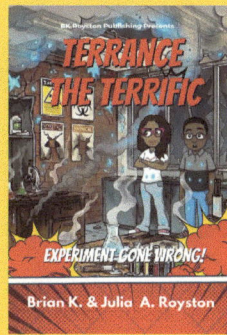

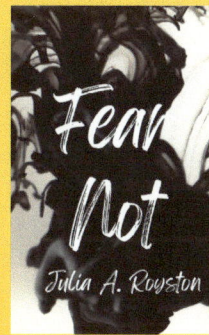

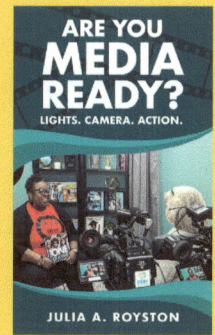

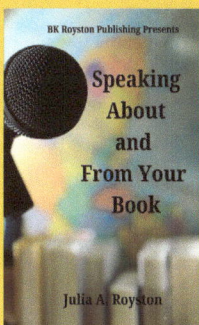

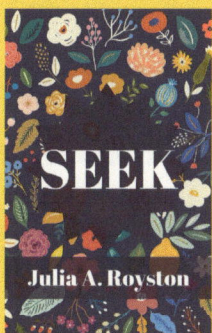

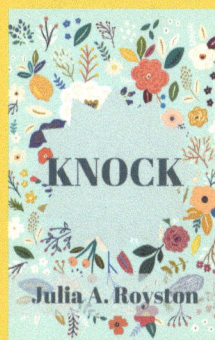

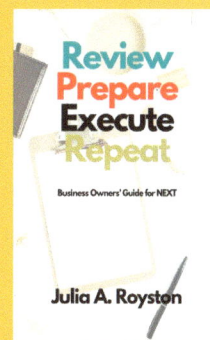

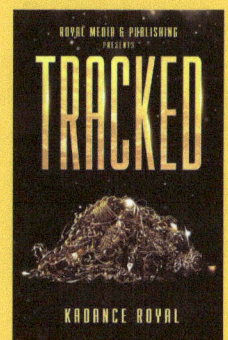

Purchase:

www.roystonroyalbookstore.com

Julia A. Royston
Books Available at These Stores and Book Fairs

www.roystonchildrenbookstore.com

www.roystonroyalbookstore.com

Next Chapter Bookstore
Greensboro, NC

When I See Me Book Fair

The Amazing Corner

Sankofa Center Bookstore at Bates Memorial
Louisville, KY

The Garden of Readin Book Closet
Indianapolis, IN

AVAILABLE AUDIOBOOKS!

Fiction

Coming Soon!

Contact Us

🌐
Websites
For Publishing:
www.talkwithroyston.com
www.juliaakroyston.com

🌐
Email Address
bkroystonpublishing@gmail.com
royalmediapublishing@gmail.com

📞
Phone
502.694.2143

AUDIOBOOKS NOW AVAILABLE

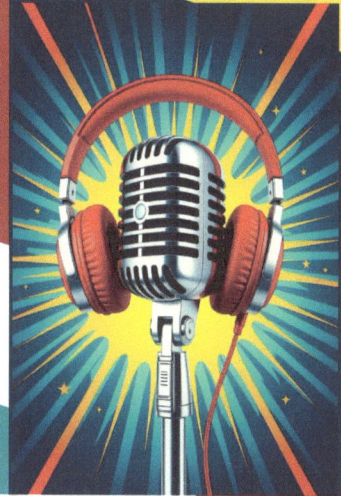

About Us

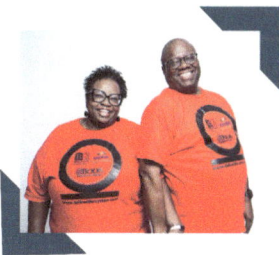

BK Royston Publishing was established in 2008 and Royal Media and Publishing was established in 2015. Both of these companies are full service book publishing companies. Take the author from the idea in their head through the publishing process and beyond. With nearly combined publishing experience of 20+ years, we have been able to publish more than 450+ books and there are many more to come.

Children's Audiobooks

Adult Audiobooks

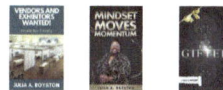

Royston Strategy Session

What We'll Cover:

Vision
Audience
Product Creation
Systems
Strategy
Success

Let's go!

Julia A. Royston
Author. Speaker. Consultant.

Register TODAY!!
www.roystonstrategysession.com

Relaunch Website! Check it Out Today!

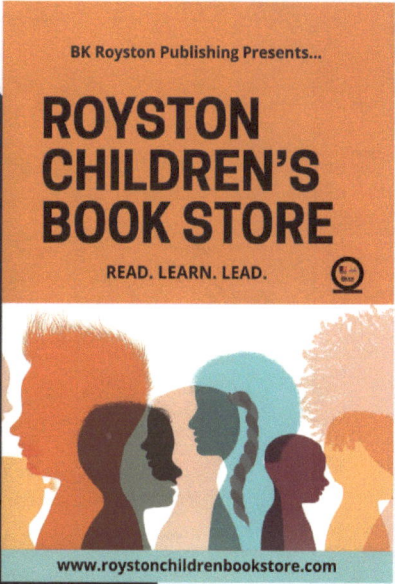

BK Royston Publishing Presents...

ROYSTON CHILDREN'S BOOK STORE

READ. LEARN. LEAD.

www.roystonchildrenbookstore.com

www.roystonchildrenbookstore.com

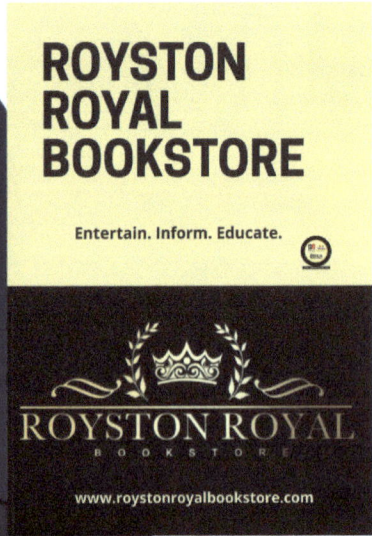

www.ingramcontent.com/pod-product-compliance
Lightning Source LLC
Chambersburg PA
CBHW052048190326
41521CB00002BA/149